S0-CYG-113

JACKIE

First published in the United States of America in 1998
by UNIVERSE PUBLISHING
A Divison of Rizzoli International Publications, Inc.
300 Park Avenue South
New York, NY 10010
and
THE VENDOME PRESS

Text and captions translated by Chanterelle Translations, London

Front cover: Jackie in Canada on her first official visit. © Stanley Tretick/Sygma.
Back cover: Souvenir-covered wall, in Caroline's room in Newport,
where the Kennedys were married. © Kraft/Sygma.

ISBN: 0-7893-0251-9

Printed and bound in Italy

Library of Congress Catalog Card Number: 98-61193

UNIVERSE OF STARS

JACKIE

By Nicole Salinger

UNIVERSE/VENDOME

"As you set out for Ithaka, hope your road is a long one full of adventure, full of discovery . . . May there be many summer mornings when, with what pleasure, what joy, you enter harbors you're seeing for the first time."

CONSTANTIN CAVAFIS, *Ithaka*

On July 14, 1989, Jackie Onassis went to Paris to attend the bicentennial celebration of the French Revolution. She watched from a balcony overlooking the Place de la Concorde, which afforded a bird's eye view of the exciting spectacle. The rue de Rivoli, located at the foot of the building, was being used as a parking lot for the official cars waiting for the heads of state. The former First Lady, with a somewhat distant expression, looked furtively upon the huge black limousine, the armored doors of which bore the U.S. presidential seal. Then she turned towards the colorful swirls of the parade. At this point, amazement and pleasure filled her large eyes and, in her unique voice, at once vivacious and breathy, she pronounced one of her trademark witty comments: "I come to Paris and I see a Broadway parade! Andy Warhol has won over General de Gaulle!"

Jackie could turn single moments into celebrations. She was overjoyed to be back in her beloved Paris on this warm summer night, and to have the opportunity to savor the commemoration of a page in French history she knew perfectly.

Despite the spontaneity and cheerfulness this elegant, intelligent woman exhibited at that moment, it was difficult not to be reminded of another image of her when, twenty-six years earlier, she had shown the world her quiet, dignified strength, in a moment of extreme duress, leaving her distinct mark on a dark chapter of U.S. history. Her reference to the apostle of pop art unmistakably recalls the painting of her grief-stricken face when, still spattered with her murdered husband's blood, she stood by the new president of the United States as he took the oath of office aboard the plane carrying the casket from Dallas to Washington DC. It was at this precise moment that the radiant spouse of the most charismatic of the American presidents, whose deeds and gestures mesmerized the masses, introduced a sense of myth to the Kennedy legend.

Never has a personality been so familiar and yet so misunderstood, so visible and so secret. A private person riding in a public caravan, this discreet woman only granted two television interviews during her three years as First Lady: one at the White House; the other, two months after the death of the president, when she thanked the hundreds of thousands of those who had expressed their sympathy.

If she refused to give interviews or write her memoirs it was because she preferred to live her life rather than talk about it. And yet, between the time when, at thirty-one, she became the youngest First Lady in the history of the United States, and her death thirty-three years later, she was placed on the cover of countless magazines (at least eighteen times for *Life*) and was the subject of hundreds of articles and dozens of books.

The press and public made her a national icon. A few years later, the legend was temporarily shattered, when she stepped out of her role of eternal widow. But, as evidenced by the public's widespread sadness at the time of her death, she had maintained her place in people's hearts.

Although the press's opinion was fickle, Jacqueline Bouvier-

Kennedy-Onassis was always the same captivating, complex woman. She was both simple and sophisticated, detached and passionate, dutiful and capricious, warm and aloof, blithe and serious, or, as one magazine summed her up, "grace and iron." As demanding of herself as she was of others, she proved to be generous and thoughtful, perhaps expressing herself best through the letters, notes, and tokens that will remain the treasures of those who knew her. Her spirit and grace lent her an unselfconscious magnetism. Truly cultivated—and taken by French culture in particular—she sensed the epic dimensions of the present would be enlightened by the history and legend of the past.

Her style had nothing to do with vanity. It was simply her singular way of living. Her elegance was not related to artifice; rather, it was an expression of her vision of beauty and her conviction that art was the essence of life. These words uttered by Socrates could have been about her: "Love is the desire to be born again through beauty."

But, more than anything else, her children—Caroline and John—were at the heart of Jackie's concerns: "If you bungle raising your children, nothing else much matters in life," she once observed. And she did not bungle.

The East Coast and Europe

As in the fairy tales she devoured as soon as she was able to read, Jacqueline Lee Bouvier had a golden childhood on the large estates her family owned along the east coast of the United States. She was born on July 28, 1929, three months before the Wall Street crash in which her father, John Bouvier would lose a good part of his fortune. A descendant of a French soldier who had served under Napoleon I, "Black Jack" was a dark, handsome, whimsical man, with a weakness for women and drink. It was to him that Jackie owed her affinity for France and the penchant for elegance which inspired her life. Her mother, Janet Lee, daughter of a New York banker, was a perfect hostess whose social gatherings Jackie preferred to escape in order to read, draw, and listen to music.

Jackie was eleven when her parents divorced. This would be the first wound she would heal by taking refuge in an imaginary world where she could invent a marvelous future.

Horses were her passion. She took solace in long horseback rides at Merrywood estate in Virginia, where her mother lived with her new husband, the very wealthy Hugh Auchincloss. The horse shows and the dressage taught her never to override, to hold her reins with style, gently but firmly.

In Newport, elected "debutante of the year," she was described in the local paper as a superb brunette with classic features and a complexion as delicate as Dresden porcelain.

She was a liberal arts major at Vassar College, a university for high-society girls. In New York, her essay on "People I wish I had known" won the *Vogue* Magazine Prix de Paris essay contest. She chose Charles Baudelaire and Oscar Wilde as her subjects, because they were "poets and idealists who could paint their sinfulness with honesty, and still believe in something higher"; and Serge Diaghilev, because "he possessed what is rarer than artistic genius—the sensitivity to take the best in each man and incorporate it into a masterpiece." And she wrote, "If I could be sort of overall art director of the twentieth century, it would be their theories of art that I would apply to my period. . ."

At eighteen, she set out on her first trip to Europe. She fell in love with France, the land of her ancestors. A year's study at the Sorbonne gave her a perfect mastery of French, which later enabled her to charm General de Gaulle and André Malraux. Soon after, she returned to France and visited Italy and Spain with her sister Lee. Together, they assembled an elaborate scrapbook and diary written and illustrated with subtlety and humor. Lee, who was to become Princess Radziwill, would publish it in 1974 under the title *One Special Summer.*

Her first job as "Inquiring Camera Girl" for the Washington *Times-Herald*, brought her to Washington DC where she met John Kennedy, the young and dashing senator from Massachusetts who was twelve years her elder. While in London covering the coronation of Queen Elizabeth, she received a telegram signed by John Kennedy: "Articles excellent, but you are missed. . ." Upon her return, they got engaged. Later on, Kennedy joked that it was safer to marry Jackie and remove her from the Fourth Estate becasue she was becoming too much a risk to his political fortunes.

From Massachusetts to Washington DC

Jackie easily won the hearts of the Kennedy family. At the Kennedy compound in Hyannis Port on Cape Cod, she tried her hand at touch football, a game that brought out the Kennedys' competitive edge. She enchanted Joe, the father of the family, in particular, with her charm and intellect. Although she might have dreamed of a more discreet wedding, crowds lined up as twelve hundred guests from the world of politics, finance, and society filled St. Mary's Church and attended the reception at her parents' summer home in Newport on the beautiful sunny afternoon of September 12, 1953. Jacqueline Kennedy realized that she was marrying a "whirlwind," and the Kennedy family knew that she would be a major asset in future electoral campaigns. During the honeymoon in Acapulco, she wrote a poem to her husband:

". . . Now he was here with the wind and the sea
And all the things he was going to be . . .
he would find love
he would never find peace
For he must go seeking
The Golden Fleece. . . "

J. F. K. and his wife shared a passion for history. Bed-bound for several months after a back operation following a war injury, he found his wife to be a precious partner in writing *Profiles in Courage*, which won him the Pulitzer prize. He was drawn to her interest in art and literature; she admired his lively spirit and constantly inquiring mind.

To prepare for the duties that awaited her, she took political science courses at Georgetown University. And although she was more attracted to museums and intimate dinner parties than to platforms and political rallies, she plunged into the presidential campaign wholeheartedly. Keeping a tight rein on her shyness, she never hesitated to greet the public and shake hands: crowds rushed to see her.

In January 1960, two months after the presidential campaign was formally launched, she learned that she was pregnant for the second time. Caroline was two years old at the time. Her doctor ordered her to stay close to home. From there, she answered mail, taped TV spots, and wrote a syndicated column, "Campaign Wife." The day after J. F. K. won the nomination in Los Angeles, she was swamped by reporters in her house in Hyannis Port.

On November 9, 1960, John Fitzgerald Kennedy became the thirty-fifth president of the United States of America, winning by a narrow margin. Two weeks later, aboard his plane, the *Caroline*, with potential members of his future government, the president elect learned of the birth of his son John. Jacqueline Kennedy would have barely two months to prepare herself for the inauguration and the move to the White House, on January 20, 1961. From this day on, her family life would be in the public spotlight.

The White House

The Kennedys settled into the White House at a time when the lack-luster postwar years were easing into an era of peace and prosperity. This "New Frontier" strengthened American aspirations to defend freedom at home and abroad. Upon entering this age of "poetry and power," as it was described by the poet Robert Frost at the inauguration ceremony, the American dream was finding a new impulse.

Jacqueline Kennedy set out to transform the nation's capital and the White House into a benchmark of excellence, a source of inspiration and pride for all Americans.

Her first priority, however, was to create a refuge where her children and husband could lead as normal a family life as possible. She renovated the private appartments, including the children's nursery, where she created a kindergarten for both her own and the White House staff's children.

The American imagination was immediately captivated by irresistible scenes that portrayed John and Caroline playing in the Oval Office with the most powerful man in the world. At this point, Jackie declared war on the press's invasiveness; their relentless curiosity and aggressive tactics completely disregarded the boundaries she had established between her private and public life. She bombarded the president's press secretary with outraged notes: "Pierre, I thought that you had made an agreement with the press not to photograph the children playing at the White House. They have had all the pictures of Macaroni (Caroline's pony) they need . . . to make him a national joke . . . It is not fair to Caroline . . . What is a press secretary for—to help the press, yes—but also to protect us . . ." It was a lost battle; these images would be published the world over and would only serve to fortify the Kennedy legend.

Jackie devoted herself wholeheartedly to the project that was dearest to her: placing culture at the center of the nation's public life. With this goal in mind, she began with the White House. Surrounding herself with museum curators, art historians, and wealthy friends, she formed the Fine Arts Committee for the White House, whose function was to restore the presidential residence to its status of historical monument.

Afterwards, she personally oversaw the production of an illustrated guide, which quickly became a best-seller; the profits went to the Fine Arts Committee. In 1962, when she agreed to give a televised tour through the White House, fifty-six million viewers suddenly developed a passion for their heritage.

Convinced that majesty is an essential quality in strong leadership, she transformed the White House into an elegant meeting place for the greatest artists and most renowned writers. Among the many was cellist Pablo Casals, who returned to the United States to give an unforgettable concert; André Malraux was so impressed by the welcome he received that he convinced the Louvre to lend the Mona Lisa to the National Gallery of Art in Washington; Isaac Stern was invited to a lunch, during which plans were made for the future Kennedy Center.

The president supported his wife's mission of excellence, even if certain dresses and antiques sometimes cost more than expected. In his speeches he would interject: "I look forward to an America which will not be afraid of grace and beauty," "This country cannot afford to be materially rich and spiritually poor," or, "I look forward to an

America which commands respect throughout the world not only for its strength but its civilization as well. . ."

He was equally proud of his wife when, during a visit to France, Jackie so enchanted General de Gaulle and the French that he introduced himself as "the man accompanying Jacqueline Kennedy." While in Vienna, Nikita Khrushchev said to journalists requesting a picture with Kennedy, "I would rather shake *her* hand."

Dallas and Arlington

After the president finished three years in office, when the time came to think about reelection and winning over reluctant states, which included Texas, Jackie decided to accompany him on his campaigning trips.

Dallas prepared a triumphant welcome for the presidential couple. Bouquets of roses and cries of welcome followed the motorcade down its course. On this November 22, 1963, the sun flooded the passengers in the black, convertible limousine. At the request of her husband, Jackie took off her sunglasses so the crowd could see her better. At 12:30, three bullet shots rang out. In the new age of television, the whole country watched as John Kennedy was shot down. America fell into a state of shock. As President Clinton would say thirty years later: "Even in the face of impossible tragedy, Jackie Kennedy carried the grief of our entire nation with a calm power." Indeed, her courage was awesome: she never left her husband's side; she did not change out of her blood-stained pink suit until she arrived back in Washington, so no one would forget the shame of the murder; she insisted on standing by Lyndon Johnson, the new president of the United States, as he took the oath of office. Although her face was rigid with sorrow as she descended the steps of Air Force One, which carried her husband's casket to Washington, she did not shed a tear.

As soon as she arrived at Andrews Air Force Base, she asked aides to research the burial of Abraham Lincoln, who had also been assassinated while in office. A committee was established in the White House. Jackie made all the decisions: the coffin would rest on a catafalque duplicating Lincoln's and be drawn by six white horses; a black riderless thoroughbred would follow; in its stirrups two boots would be turned backwards, symbolizing the death of a hero. The melancholic sound of Irish bagpipes would follow John Fitzgerald Kennedy's last voyage to Arlington National Cemetery; and an eternal flame would burn on his grave. All of America and millions of television viewers throughout the world had their eyes riveted on Jackie. No one would forget Jackie's dignity when she got down on her knees, with her six-year-old daughter Caroline, to kiss her husband's casket; when she told John to give his father a military salute; when she led the procession to St. Matthew's Cathedral, surrounded by family and followed by world leaders; when she hugged against her heart the neatly folded American flag that had covered the casket.

With extraordinary strength, she was able to contain the sorrow that overcame America and the world. Jackie had fulfilled her commitment to her husband, her children, and her country.

After Dallas

The new White House residents were extremely thoughtful towards Jackie Kennedy, leaving her all the time she needed to move out and settle into the house that the Harrimans had lent her in Washington. "Lyndon Johnson felt so bad for me that I almost felt sorry for him." She only had two requests: that the space center in Florida be renamed

"Cape Kennedy," and that the renovation of the capital be continued. Johnson offered to appoint her ambassador to Paris. She appreciated the offer, but declined.

Before leaving the White House for the last time, she wrote letters to numerous people, not forgetting the widow of the police officer killed in Dallas on that November 22. She also offered a personal Kennedy souvenir to each member of her husband's staff.

But mostly she looked after her children: "It is the children who enable widows to go on," she once said. Later, Caroline, who was to become one of the directors of the Kennedy Foundation, noted that while most people talked to her about the tragic loss of her father, she and her family were more concerned about celebrating his life.

Two months after Dallas, Jackie appeared on television to thank all those who had expressed their affection and sympathy, and announced plans to build the Kennedy Library. It would store the archives of a presidency that had been brief but intense. She organized an exhibit of John Kennedy's mementos that would travel throughout the United States and abroad.

She then settled in New York, in an apartment that looked out onto the Metropolitan Museum of Art, and over Central Park's changing seasons. Here, the world would finally respect her privacy, and she only came out of her isolation to support her brother-in-law, Robert Kennedy, in his presidential campaign. She also made the most of the newfound calm she was enjoying by traveling.

But barely five years had gone by when assassins' bullets struck again. On April 4, 1968, Martin Luther King was shot down in Memphis, Tennessee; on June 6, her brother-in-law Robert Kennedy was killed in Los Angeles after winning the California primaries which would have opened his way to the White House. Robert Kennedy had been Jackie's friend and a source of support. He had held her hand during her husband's funeral. They had read the Greek poets together. The nightmare was to start all over again. On board the same Air Force One, Jackie accompanied the casket of yet another Kennedy to Washington; and she returned to Arlington Cemetery for another burial. Her children's safety now became her main preoccupation and she decided finally to flee the dark shadow of violence and mourning.

Greece

America had expected her to remain a widow forever. But, at thirty-nine, Jackie Kennedy wanted to live some more. When the Greek shipping magnate Aristotle Onassis offered her both a moral and a material exile, she gratefully accepted. Onassis had been a guest at the White House and Jackie had been a guest on the *Christina*, his magnificent yacht on which she had sought refuge to recover from the death of her prematurely born son Patrick in August 1963. Fascinated and comforted by Onassis, Jacqueline Kennedy flew with her children to his island, Skorpios, where the couple were married on October 20, 1968. This marriage, for which her brother-in-law, Ted Kennedy, drew up the agreement, struck the American public as an act of betrayal. Suddenly she was as vehemently criticized as she had been idolized.

Those who only saw Onassis for his millions didn't really know this short, stocky man, who was neither handsome nor distinguished-looking. And yet his charisma, lively spirit, and talent for telling stories had already captivated such public world figures as Winston Churchill and Maria Callas. He had built his own empire, and Jackie seemed to be drawn to uncommon men. But she also projected her fascination with Greece onto him. Onassis was Greek; that is, from the country that invented both tragedy and poetry. Had she ever traced a parallel between Ulysses, the wandering hero of a thousand journeys, whose adventures she loved to read in the *Odyssey*, and her husband, born in Smyrna, not far from Troy, who lived on his boat, and whose private island of Skorpios was within sight of Ithaka. . .? Ari, as his friends called him, allowed her to spend happy days in genuine peace. He was a thoughtful stepfather for her children, showing off his country to them, including the excavations at Santorini in which Jackie took a particular interest. But her new life triggered waves of assaults from the paparazzi who became increasingly more intrusive. The tranquility of Skorpios was spoiled. A trial ensued and she won a court ruling against a particularly ruthless photographer who was ordered to stay 25 feet from her, and 30 feet from her children.

The magic between Jackie and Ari gradually wore off as their interests began to diverge. Even remarried, Jackie remained, at heart, a Kennedy. When Aristotle Onassis died in Paris in 1975, she decided to return to the United States, where her second husband had never really been accepted.

New York

Here, Jacqueline Onassis spent the last eighteen years of her life. Finally, she led a normal life, on her own terms, far from the turbulence of public life. She would, however, never shy away from keeping the memory of her husband alive, inaugurating, for example, the Kennedy Library designed by her friend I. M. Pei, on the Boston harbor.

Her children grew up well-equipped to face life. She was a proud and happy mother who attended their college graduations, and also Caroline's wedding, which was celebrated in June 1986, in Hyannis Port, with the whole Kennedy family.

Her passion for books led her to Viking Press, where she worked as an editor until she learned of a novel that was to be published about the assassination of Ted Kennedy. She resigned that very day. She then went to Doubleday, where she edited up to a dozen books a year, distinguishing herself by her professionalism, discerning knowledge, and her modesty.

She also dedicated herself to several humanitarian and artistic causes, and assumed a leading role in the preservation of monuments and sites.

It seems that Jackie finally found peace in her final years, which she spent in the company of Maurice Tempelsman, a caring, cultivated companion with whom she went on morning walks through Central Park, on rides in Virginia, and on ocean outings. They were seen at Carnegie Hall and in France—her last trip. She also took great joy in the presence of her three grandchildren.

The woman who had captivated the world with her intelligence, elegance, and grace passed away on May 19, 1994, at her New York home, surrounded by her family and friends. Remembering this dignified, unflappable woman with great respect and affection, the people of America followed her to her grave in Arlington National Cemetery, where she rests beside John Fitzgerald Kennedy.

"Jackie was too young to be a widow in 1963 and too young to die now," said Ted Kennedy. "She would have preferred to be just herself, but the world insisted she be a legend too. . ."

Chronology

1929: July 28. Jacqueline Lee Bouvier is born in East Hampton, Long Island, New York. She is the daughter of Janet Lee Bouvier and John Vernon Bouvier III, a successful Wall Street broker. Her childhood is spent between New York City and East Hampton.

1942: After divorcing in 1940, Jacqueline's mother marries Hugh D. Auchincloss II. The family moves to Merrywood, Auchincloss's estate near Washington DC.

1943–46: Attends Miss Porter's school for girls in Connecticut.

1947–48: Named "Debutante of the Year."

1951: Studies at Vassar College. She spends her junior year traveling in France and takes classes at the Sorbonne.

1952: Jacqueline is hired as "Inquiring Camera Girl" for the Washington *Times-Herald*. She meets John Fitzgerald Kennedy, thirty-four-year-old Massachusetts senator, considered one of the most eligible bachelors of the moment.

1953: Following their engagement in July, Jacqueline and Jack are featured on the cover of *Life* magazine. The wedding takes place on September 12, at St. Mary's Church, Newport. More than a thousand guests attend the reception given at Auchincloss's estate. The young couple moves to Georgetown, Washington DC.

1957: Birth of Caroline Bouvier Kennedy.

1960–61: In January 1960, John Fitzgerald Kennedy declares his candidacy to the presidency. Elected on November 9, he takes the oath of office on January 20, 1961, becoming the thirty-fifth president of the United States of America. On November 25, 1960, Jackie gives birth to John Fitzgerald Kennedy, Jr. The Kennedys move into the White House.

1961: Jackie devotes herself to her children, protecting them from the press and the public. She sets out to restore the White House, raising funds from private donations, and oversees the publication of a White House guidebook. She triumphs at the numerous state banquets and receptions which form part of her life as First Lady.

1962 : In February, Jackie Kennedy opens the doors of the White House to CBS television and gives a guided tour which is watched by fifty-six million viewers.

Jackie Kennedy and General de Gaulle, who was impressed as much by her beauty and charm as her fluent French and knowledge of French history (1961). © Archive Photos.

1963: August 7, Patrick Bouvier Kennedy is born prematurely. He dies a few days later. On November 22, John Fitzgerald Kennedy is killed in Dallas.

1964: In September, Jackie moves with her children to an apartment at 1040 Fifth Avenue, New York.

1968: Martin Luther King is assassinated on April 4; Robert Kennedy on June 6. On October 20, Jackie marries the Greek shipping magnate, Aristotle Onassis, twenty-three years her senior.

1975: Onassis dies, leaving Jackie a substantial fortune.

1979: Commissioned at Jackie's initiative, the John Fitzgerald Kennedy Library is formally opened. Designed by I. M. Pei, it overlooks Boston harbor.

1975–94: New York. She works as an editor at Viking Press (1975-1977), and then at Doubleday (1977-1994).

1994: May 19, Jackie dies at her New York home. She is laid to rest beside John Fitzgerald Kennedy, at Arlington National Cemetery, outside of Washington DC.

Jackie

Five-year-old Jackie with her parents at the annual horse show organized by the Southampton Riding and Hunt Club. © Sipa Press.

Vacation in Ravello (Italy), where she went with her daughter in August 1962 to spend a couple of days in a house rented by her sister. Benno Graziani, a friend and reporter at *Paris Match*, stands behind her. © Benno Graziani.
Jackie at sixteen, posing like a starlet, at the Newport tennis club. © Magnum.

Jackie learned to ride before she learned to speak. Her jumping classes won her her first show ribbons at the age of six. © Archive Photos/Morgan.

Jackie was a lively, intelligent child, but bossy and quite difficult, according to her nanny. © Archive Photos/Morgan.
With John, Jr., age three, on the beach at their house in Hyannis Port, Massachusetts, where the whole Kennedy family spent their summers.
© Stanley Tretick/Sygma.

With Caroline, in Hyannis Port. Jackie always tried to ensure that her children led a healthy, happy life, as little disturbed by the status of their parents as possible.
© Archive Photos.
Charmed by the young Massachusetts senator in the early 1950s, Jackie joins him in Hyannis Port, at the Kennedy home on the Ocean. © Archive Photos.

On September 12, 1953, Jacqueline Bouvier marries John Fitzgerald Kennedy at her parents' estate in Newport. Among the fourteen ushers, Teddy and Bobby, brothers of the groom, flank the radiant couple. © Archive Photos/Tal.

The wedding cake was a gift from a Massachusetts baker, a democrat. © Sygma.

Jackie at a cocktail party, during the 1950s. © Archive Photos/Bert Morgan.

A time for the Kennedys to relax, in 1963, in the country house they had rented in Virginia, not far from Washington DC. © Magnum.

March 1962. After a ten-day visit in India, Jackie and her sister, Lee Radziwill, discover Pakistan, its culture and customs. Here they're pictured riding a dromedary. © Archive Photos/Tal.

Ravello, Italy, August 1961. Jackie takes Caroline to church on Sunday. © Benno Graziani.

Jackie in England at her sister Lee Radziwill's, with her nephew Anthony and niece Christina on Christmas Day, 1968. © Benno Graziani.

A huge crowd surrounds the presidential couple. © Stanley Tretick/Sygma.

The Kennedys visit to Paris in June 1961 was a triumph for Jackie. Here she is pictured leaving the Quai d'Orsay, where she stayed with her husband. © Archive Photos.

Warm welcome in Ravello, August 1962, where Jackie and her daughter Caroline met up with Jackie's sister, Princess Radziwill, seen here with her son Anthony. © Archive Photos.

On a sunny Autumn morning, November 22, 1963, the presidential couple arrives at Dallas's Love Field Airport, welcomed by a cheering crowd. © J. F. K. Library/Sygma.

Jackie Kennedy's elegance and style was to give America a new image. Photo taken in June 1961. © Archive Photos.

January 20, 1961, John Fitzgerald Kennedy is sworn in as the thirty-fifth president of the United States of America—and the youngest president ever to be elected in the nation's history. © J. F. K. Library/Sygma.

Jackie's first official visit was to Canada, where the Parliament applauded her with more spirit than they did the Queen of England. © Stanley Tretick/Sygma.

Hyannis Port, Massachusetts, is the Kennedy family's meeting place. Here, little John is flanked by his mother and uncle Bobby. © Stanley Tretick/Sygma.

Summer 1959. Jackie relaxes in Hyannis Port. © Sygma.

On May 31, 1961, the presidential couple arrives in Paris. Jackie's elegance and knowledge of the French language and culture would help to make this official visit a resounding success. © Archive Photos.
After her visit to India and Pakistan, in March 1962, Jackie made a short, three-day stopover in London, to visit her sister. During this time she lunched at Buckingham Palace. © Archive Photos.

Calm determination. © Archive Photos.
April 4, 1966. Jackie, Caroline, and John, about to fly out of Kennedy Airport to spend Easter vacation in Argentina. © Archive Photos.

Unwillingly, Jackie aroused incessant public curiosity. The paparazzi swooped down on her when she married Aristotle Onassis. New York, March 1975. © Ron Galella/Sygma.
Resplendent, Jackie ruled over the White House, turning it into the most sophisticated social meeting place in the world. © J. F. K. Library/Sygma.

Jackie 1963, one of the works she inspired Andy Warhol to paint (1 x 1 m). © Adagp, Paris 1998.